POETRY

VOLCANO SMOKE AT DIAMOND BEACH

JEREMY REED

Volcano Smoke at Diamond Beach

Cloudforms No. 6

Cloudforms are published by CLOUD
48 Biddlestone Road, Heaton
Newcastle upon Tyne NE6 5SL

Series Editor: Michael Thorp

This collection © CLOUD 1992
Poems © Jeremy Reed 1992
Photograph © John Robinson 1992

All Rights Reserved

ISBN 0 9514457 5 8

Typeset by True North
Printed by Tyneside Free Press

Acknowledgements

I am grateful to the Musées Royaux des Beaux-Arts de Belgique, Brussels, for permission to incorporate 'La Partition Complète Complétée' by E.L.T. Mesens (1945) in the cover design; and to John Robinson for permission to include his photograph of the author as frontispiece.

My thanks to Jeremy Reed for his caring involvement in the preparation of this book, and his faith in all that is yet to be imagined; and to my wife, Frances, without whom, I can't imagine.

Contents

9   The Castle
10 Starfish in the Sky
11 Hart Crane
13 Convolvulus
14 Wedding
15 Zamora Institute
16 Lying Down (after Robert Desnos 'Couchée')
17 Star-Map
18 Scarlet Begonias and Blue Thoughts
19 Camping
20 Light as it Apprehends Red Panthers
21 Snapdragons
22 You Were Wearing Red
23 By Way of Being Here
24 Red Carnations
25 Big Shifts
26 Looking Down
27 Footnotes
28 Seasons
29 Nasturtiums
30 Taxi to the End of the World
31 Suicide Bridge
32 Rites of Passage
33 White

The Castle

We built it out of paper on the road,
stopping off where a place seemed to invite
distinction by a mulberry tree,

a red rose bordered vineyard where the grapes
waxed heavily in black ringlets, a mood
somewhere that fitted with our own
speculations, building with grey paper
not stones, and writing poetry
on walls we would assemble in the end
if we could find the spot.

It wasn't Kafka's castle, something else,
no crenellations, turrets, dark green moats
or rooks ragging into the wind
up high. No torture cells, interrogation rooms,
automatized bureaucracy.

We built by fragments, without a blueprint
on squares of paper. Later we'd meet up
with artists, draughtsmen who would illustrate
our progress. Ladders in the sky
were there for communication.
The harvest was red-gold. The mauve grapes fat.
A woman we encountered on the road
had sleepwalked out of a painting.
We carried on. We had our work to do,
and were the last survivors of a lost nation.

Starfish in the Sky

Where the last sentence stopped, I'd meant to write
how there were children sat under red umbrellas
in rainy woods after their mushroom feast,
as though I'd strayed to the interior
of a poem by Desnos, found the gold
lodged in an owl's hole and a lost poem
placed in the toe-piece of a silk stocking
hung from a branch, and the abandoned car
still bubbling in the lake; the two down there

making aquatic love. I'd pulled the line
abruptly short on action, how it all
goes on, begins again when we would stop,
and now demands I walk across a field
to the end of the world. White breakers, stone,
a naked woman waving a red scarf
at the blue sky. The children stay behind;
they're high on mushrooms and not wanted here,
but one sits watching from a height,
and lines a paper starfish as a kite
into the wind. This is a stopping point,
another break in narrative. Black clouds
are building. It must be the coming night?

Hart Crane

The big push, manic overdrive, Hart Crane
in South Street, Sand Street, cruising for sailors,
his pocketbook blotched by whiskey, night rain
to inky thumbprints, doodled stars and stripes
and love-hearts. A gangster suit, orange tie,
he feeds off his reckless dichotomy –
the tempestuous visionary who hypes

his disordered senses until they push
language to the ruthless frontiers of sex,
and then by day at Sweets, slowing the rush,
the advertizing copy clerk still hung over,
a cheroot snaking smoke into his eye,
and Grace and Grandma demanding letters
in his lunchbreaks. He is a cooked lobster,

hard-shelled already, a grey brush of hair
outgrown the black; rashed vesicles, a wild
impulsive maudit swinging on the air
of New York jazz, imploding poetry
to Ravel's Bolero, played sixty times
to heighten mania; and how the power was there
in the compressed, metaphoric vitality

to stand out as distinctly new, a way
of having the poem hold up and keep
a skyscraper view of the century.
Pugnacious, dangerous as a Russian bear
when overlit, thrown in a Paris jail,
dusted by New York cops, Hart's mad rampage
burnt out his gift. We feel his late despair,

poetic impotence, his poverty
unrelieved by his father's candy Life Saver,
his volcanic storms shaking white-hot ash
over his friends. His style was to sever

with every obstruction, give up the page
for self-debasement, kneeling down to blow
some anonymous, car-parking stranger,

and violently shipping out from the States
for a tequila-fired nerve-jab at Mexico,
it seemed the inevitable exit,
a last desiccated fish-gasp to write
the vision down; and reversed, coming back
he tilted overboard at noon, his white
shirt puffed before the water smacked it slack.

Convolvulus

A mid-year turning point, familiar,
proclaiming Georgia O'Keefe's New York,

their voluted corollas are funnels
chased out of nettle proliferation;

and they refer me to my need to earth
volatilized nerves: I had forgotten

their bitter earth smell; it is wild lettuce
or stone approved olfactory,

and it's high June, and yet they're September,
white flags amongst spoofed blackberries . . .

And it's a trick of the mind to think back
to what's there when they aren't, and memory

that rarely gets the details right
invents surprises. Triangular flowers,

a dream in the shape of a box
in which an eye selects its colour rods.

But now they're here and loll plattered
like decapitations. A smoky dust

lifts with a puff of wind. Convolvulus
is what it says and means in that syntax

of granulated flurries. I must catch
their season and that is a form of trust.

Wedding

A green peacock on a black beach.
The sunbather snorts a line of cocaine
and is his own music: not Station to Station
heard again in a new decade
somewhere in Europe after morning rain,
a door open on a white chiffon bride
anxious for the arrival of a car

to take her there.
The wave has beached an empty coffin,
strewn it with a soggy red weed.
The sunbather is waiting for someone;
he wears a sequinned face-veil
for the wedding.
                        They'll marry by the tide,

the black car waiting for them in the dunes.

Zamora Institute

He inserts a mauve contact lens and checks
his reconstructed features; collagen
implants, liposuction; he's angular
and out-profiles Michael Jackson.
Outside, a metal tree shaped like a star

scintillates in the dangerous UV light.
A child sits in a sculpted conifer
and walkie-talkies his robotic toy.
The real park lions are lobotomized.
The big one sleeps curled up on a parked car.

And daily, new arrivals come to stay
and attend lectures. They will recreate
themselves; dismantle knowledge of their past,
adopt names given by their instructors
and stand outside a compression-sealed gate

awaiting admission into a cult
for the re-formed. No-one may ever speak
of the initiation. Some remain
inside for years and return as children
who walk off fearless across a dust plain

towards the lost cities; the fabled worlds
where earlier ancestors lived and died.
He checks his memory loss on a screen,
the red digits read cancelled and the green
matter to be revised. The optimum

is 0.5 green. And still the children play
their adult games before lectures, and ten
analysands strike out beneath the trees,
headed for pre-initiation jabs
they walk clean through the sleeping lion's den.

Lying Down
after Robert Desnos 'Couchée'

To the right, the sky, to the left, the sea.
And in front of you, the grass and its flowers.
A cloud, the road follows its vertical way
Parallel to the plumbline of the horizon,
Parallel to the rider.
The horse bolts towards its imminent fall
And the other climbs interminably.
Everything seems so simple and unreal.
Lying on my left side,
I take no interest in the landscape
And I think only of imprecise things,
Very vague and very happy,
Like the tired looks you leave float free
Through this beautiful summer afternoon
To the right, to the left,
Here, there,
In the delirium of uselessness.

Star-Map

A purple curtain's drawn in the white house
opposite. An invading clump of trees
is often the dark blue-green that Magritte
uses to lodge a crescent moon
in foreshortened perspective.
                        'We're like that,'
you say, 'we blank out visuals for the surety
of space we turn to secrecy;
and what will happen if we go too far
inside the private fantasies
with which we instruct each other?' A star
is visible above their house,
a mineral starfish twinkling glacially.
It's the coming of a compact blue night.

They've left a red chair on the balcony
where she suns in the afternoon, dress off,
dark glasses, a minimal bikini.
Beyond that house the air is wider still
for no obstruction – it is grass country,
a wind that smells of horses. We let in the dark

and watch their screened off privacy.
Later, we'll revert to parameters
which are our own confinement, and pretend
we can still see their house and beyond that
a star-map open to a conjectural end.

Scarlet Begonias and Blue Thoughts

Their red's so excruciatingly brilliant –
the scarlet begonias, meringue-seashells
floppily open like full peonies

and private; coloured that way by the light;
they take the eye there; but my thoughts are blue
in meeting their solar target.
And other things are happening. She's there
my distracted neighbour, always alone
and sunning on a balcony,
a Euro-Japanese, eyes averted,
a white scarf in her blueblack hair.
She reads. Her eyelashes are butterflies.

I take in spaces of being alive;
I need so much and so little and both
are disproportionate. She goes inside
and draws a bedroom curtain, a green swish
that has her naked, while I hunt for clues
as to why red flowers dramatically
evoke a down-mood evening-blues.

Camping

Black lava blocks litter the sand. She reads
a hologrammic letter. He's absorbed
in a mid-seventies Ballard,
the solitary schizoid protagonist
in pursuit of disembodied sex,
Monroe, Elizabeth Taylor.

They've parked their helicopter on the dunes;
red ibis spill on the polluted lake,
a big scarlet umbrella of dead birds
scumming the surface. Back of them and higher up
someone's built out of planetary bits
an observatory. They can see the man
telescoped into depth-space. He has lost
all notion of the earth; his body's thin
as a stood upright laser.
He only lives on purified strawberry soda.

The two are out here camping; and indifferent
to the earth's authentic breakdown,
pursue leisure activities. They are
alone in the unfamiliar. A star
is burning greenly overhead.

They fly back to wherever is their town.

Light as it Apprehends Red Panthers

He looks up from a book. They've been away
two months, the blonde boy and his girl who speaks
to what's inanimate, a vase, a chair,
the pastel gradations in a Paul Klee,
the things that express what we haven't found
in or around ourselves, but seem to say
they're eloquently silent. When they call,

the two are there without warning, he brings
a sun-tan from the beaches, she a flower
she places in the fruit bowl as a complement
to harmonies. What do they want with him?
To browse, and feel a quality
they might get from swimming in warm shallows
off Poros, Agena, aquamarine
insinuations of the tide; a depth
in which to bask, a sort of continent
to be explored; the landmarks his, not theirs,
a sensitive austerity
in which the spaces are for working thought,
a highly charged and personal element
composed around his days, elastic hours
in which allegorical red panthers
hunt through his pages, and the couple are
just as they are although they'll never know
themselves as realities, right way up
on a beach somewhere pointing to a star.

Snapdragons

A fleshy principle
corolla on a hinge,
the popper snaps open
on a throat that's more

a fish's whale's or shark's
precisional clamp, bonnet-lock;
a lick of orange pollen
dusting the inside

Mostly they're all Summer
a glowering tiger-red
lemon or port-crimson
crackling tetchily with bees

little loaded volcanoes
vulvas open for the fit
and the encapsulated fur
is constrained like an astronaut

head-first in the tube.
They are bright-tip metaphors
of the leonine poem –
summer burning to russet

in a kiln-blaze, papery
snapdragons Septembering
as referential points to days
in which we burnt, loved and consumed

our passionate impulse to live,
honey in our throats, a song
escaped from a broken stone
telling of things still to arrive.

You Were Wearing Red

They're written into time; no longer names
but happenings, and they turn up again
dead or alive, we're never sure
in the encounter. I was on a bridge

and quite mistook someone for you
right to the eye-points and the blue
Burberry with its collar up.
The river smell had climbed into the rain

making me think of Spring and white lilacs
and how so much experientially
drifts wide of keeping. All the faces known,
internalized, burnt-in, incremented

are on constellated recall;
and those I haven't seen change, where are they
this instant, any instant, different
or dead and unknown to themselves back here

as people I don't know, crossing this bridge
in the copper-green haze to catch a train
or meet a lover? And there's nothing shows.
You wore a red dress last time, now a green;

the seasons haven't changed; the give-aways
are in the flashbacks. 'No, I wasn't late,
that was another time, that long ago
it seems just yesterday; another date . . .'

The shower returns. Moody atmospherics
shut down the screen. I'm one to one, and head
for shelter on the other side;
and the girl waiting there, is wearing red.

By Way of Being Here

They're always there as associations,
the houses that we left, the strained faces
that disappeared while looking under trees
or through a windy sheet hung up to dry
in a front garden; some of them were friends
and others strangers; others half a fruit
that didn't fit with ours, too many seeds
or an imbalanced too little? a sky
indifferently tent-pitched overhead,
the colour of blue paper with a cloud
dabbing its substance like one in Rousseau,

a sort of observer seen by the eye
to spatialize the story, populate
its drift across the inner dimensions,
the psychic continents; and where a gate
stood open on a bushed cottage, its pink
walls bleached by sunlight, there a mother watched
a son go out into the world,
not looking back despite the tidal wave
running to meet him, lifting up the dog
asleep on the country platform, drowning
a way of life inherited from small,
benign simplicities; recalling what? –
a spot on which the sunlight fell
into his room, an urge to up and go,
perversely disorder a way of life,
because we need the breakage, the fractured window
to startle us to the increasing gain
won by experience, and turning round
as we so often do, look through the glass
at what's unreachable, the Summer day
we really left at noon, stepping over
a cat, one green eye open in the grass.

Red Carnations

She balances on silver stilettos;
the floor's a mirror. If this was a dream
my eyes wouldn't blink in the reflection,
she tells herself. The music's by Satie:
she thinks of a man walking back at night
across the Paris bridges and his theme
is played by waterlights.

                And the black drape,
she goes behind it and the cubicle
opens out to a room and then a corridor.
Her bronze skirt's lighter than a butterfly;
there are no mirrors but she knows herself
going somewhere; her heels are reassuringly
a sound that substitutes for rain

which has arrived outside, a blue-brown rain
enveloping the countryside.
The chateau is still lit. It's 4 a.m.
Each window stands out like a square white moon.
A shawl of dark woods move behind.

She comes out of the corridor
and walks towards the house and there's no rain on her.
She carries red carnations. A white owl
flies out of the open door.

Big Shifts

The coast's magenta. There's a yellow hut
couched on the sands in a reality
translated out of Paul Klee's small harbour,

no swimmers anywhere, the sea
an oyster coloured watered-silk. 'It's ten
o' clock,' he says, 'in any century,
not mine, not yours.' And she looks into space,
expecting clock hands on the sun,
the punctual aircraft to arrive,
bringing them news of how the others live
in Yellow Chasm, Diamond Falls, Sirocco Road.

They pick up starfish, a folded Le Monde
used as a prop for a sunbather's head.
The date's been bleached out by the sun.
That was when people read the days
as continuity. They sit and wait:

she eats a yellow pear, watches him swim,
and anyhow the plane is late.

Looking Down

On the oak-brow, listening through antlered trees
to the source at the valley's floor;
a yellow ribbon gartered round a snake
a book open on a horse's back
nervous under maples;
the wind reading consecutive pages

to a red haired girl sitting in front of a door
that opens into a story

where the lovers meet beneath a black peacock's tail
and the stream is a vertical rainbow
guarding the way to the centre
to the luminous interior.

I brace myself in the light and the wind
dusting a copper trail. The high
sailing clouds each carry a letter from the alphabet

into the raging marigold sunset.

Footnotes

Three women lying in a triangle
brushed by the yellow poppies near the shore,
an oak relegated to the background,

their long legs arched towards the sea,
and scorpions, lacquer-black, pincer-tailed, meshing
beside a stone, as Buñuel got
a scorpion-chapter for the lens
in l'Age d'Or. Nothing but the whoosh of surf
advancing from an emerald bay.
A visible wreck hobbling in the swell.

One wears a black rose petal as a bikini,
the second, three gold sequins placed strategically,
the third is naked. These are special days,

and there's no knowing if the world exists
around the coast, or if it's disappeared
in ways given in Footnotes: see P.3.

Seasons

And was it Summer? Red leaves on the beach
not starfish, and the light a stained-glass blue,
the indigo of columbine,
and things washed up on the sands, grouped around
for composition, conch and abalone,
a salt-bleached violin, fish vertebrae,
a scraped green Moet et Chandon
bottle, roughed up by shingle, but intact;

    a gold door

took us through, it might have been sunlight
focused as a dazzling, rectangular
window into a rock, an orange frame
we climbed through to a different place,

and there were two pink deckchairs on a dark-blue beach,
orioles perched on the carbonized stumps
of a sunk forest. A solitary blonde
stood looking out to sea, naked, in silver boots,
she kept her back to us and walked away
communing with her secret, and the orioles
followed her as a black leaf-storm
forming an undulating cape around

her body. We were turning gold.
We tracked the bird-woman up a cliff path
towards a house hidden by trees.
And was it Summer? We had come too far,
journeyed beyond the seasons and were changed,
and knew we'd never find our way back to
the window in the rock, the time and place
we knew each other and were not estranged.

Nasturtiums

A bitter, peppery scent,
and perfect for the watercolourist –
an orange sun parasoled by green leaves
that finds the yellow in the flower's eye,

much like a jacket lining seen
as intermittent splashes. Saffron silk.
Watching their leaves I think of cinema,
a Japanese street scene in Kyoto –

so many green umbrellas, and the aerial shoot
resembling undulating lily pads,
a canvas turtle marching down the street.
Nasturtiums in early autumn

glower in their orange swimsuits
redder by tones than pumpkin,
almost the colour used by Klee
as wax on his 'sealed letter'.

They're a bright incentive to learn
how visuals co-ordinate,
give a woman green hair and yellow eyes
and a nasturtium on each breast;

the rest is imagination, but her skirt
is orange satin. They open out like pansies
in a water-glass.
Their thin stems are coloured like green-hay grass.

Taxi to the End of the World

And it was nothing, so the driver said,
digesting elephant steaks or zebra,
his stomach open like a corolla
discussing protein, toxins, Manhattan,
extreme eating because the planet's dead,

and he'd be going back after this ride
to the old cities, his box apartment.
'Someone's got to stay': my presentiment
was of him looting, fisting out diamonds
from display cards. Our wheels skirted the tide

and there were cattle and a family
knee-deep in water looking for a place
to cross; a bridge sunk beneath the surface
of rising waters. We went into hills,
making a detour to meet with the sea

on the last coast. The man spoke of nomads,
straggling tribes who had marched on the desert
listening for instructions, ways to alert
themselves to power, and of politicians
making suicide-pacts on pyramids.

We passed the first shacks put up on this coast.
Numeral calculations done in blood
were wildly calligraphized on white wood.
A lion-tamer instructed his child,
a group of long-haired men sat around lost;

and here the taxi stopped, he wouldn't go
right to the end, and he was obstinate.
He spoke of dangers and he had a date
that evening; love and barbecued camel,
one of the last from a blackmarket zoo.

Suicide Bridge

The salmon pass beneath, nosing downstream
towards chattering rapids, emeralds
ground to a starburst in the spray
blended with turquoise, spilling free
in torrential decantation;

the fish braiding the current's arrowhead
and free. The suicides are numerous,
spaced out as two or three a year,
nocturnal, desperate,
hitting the swollen night water
to be dragged under by a tentacle,
shocked by the cold and held down there
inside a suffocatory tent.
Hallucinating in a sten-gun burst
of images; hyperthermia.

Pedestrians are conscious of the pull,
the assertive death-gravity
is vibrational. Its field simmers;
and no steel-support, no red safety-net
will counteract the whistling vertigo,
the spiral spreadeagles to a flat hit.

I feel the power through the balls of my feet
in crossing over, and don't check my stride
but make believe someone's waiting for me
by the news kiosk on the other side.

Rites of Passage

A voice reaches me out of the white mist –
a startling intrusion, self-enquiry,
jolting me back into immediacy . . .
All Summer I kicked round for what I'd lost,
trying to connect an ignition wire
and feel the fuel flood through on the uptake,

forcing to connect with the mains. 'It's hard',
you said, 'trying to become what you were,
the pattern's shifted and it will again.'
You carried a white shell over black rocks
and christened a pawed and tailed granite slab
the purple sphinx. Above us, a ruin,

a sailor's graveyard overrun by gorse.
Summer was like slipping spaghetti straps
from amber shoulders, leaving the dress fall
into a ragged flower crown. I was up
all night, sifting through inner material,
thinking the image-clue, the particle

might show up in isolation and gel
with my anxiety. Was it someone
I'd wronged, or was the flaw so deep in me
I'd have to journey through the underworld
to rake it out as a black pearl? The sea
sounded around the house, a blueblack bay

dissected by a lighthouse. Now the days
are gold with autumn, and I hear a voice
recalling me to myself: 'You must find
the way to what you've lost.' And the leaves fall.
I stand on the threshold. The place is huge
and someone's waiting in that spotlit hall.

White

1

    He's shooting across white Ballardian sands,
    the camera open on a mirage scene
    in which Marilyn Monroe cracks her zip,
    folds her white dress over her arm and leads
    a lover into a ruined hotel.
    The man is seen from behind; a scorpion
    tattooed on his bottom, a snake's
    a red river inked on his spine.

2

    The air's so silent it's like the inside
    of sleep: the dream is all action, no sound
    accompanies the raging fire
    burning the sleeper's house; a popping shell,
    white walls split with an earthquake's flaw.

3

    The sands again; they lift up dusty wings
    announcing storm. A fighter jet drops down.
    That's Marilyn standing in white panties
    at the open window. Her lover's gone.
    The building decomposes for the lens.

4

    White dunes. Three white dinghies turned upside down,
    the sea lost somewhere like a blue
    that memory can't recreate.
    I find the film-director sitting there,
    nursing a foot, a bloodstained boot.
    I help him up to the summit
    and we are facing another country,
    white sands behind us, and in front
    a white city built in the 23rd century.

Cloudforms

Volcano Smoke at Diamond Beach is the sixth of a unique series of individual volumes from CLOUD. A developing library of creative work from Britain and abroad that addresses itself to our sense of spiritual disorientation. Urgent contemporary work interposed with older work that has in the past been given a poor hearing, or indeed not been heard at all. Work which is resonant, relevant – necessary. Each Cloudform is individually designed according to its nature, but is integral to the vision of the series as a whole. All are numbered, limited editions.

No. 1 **Lazarus Rises** by Roger Thorp with drawings by Michael Thorp.
Edition of 350 £3.95 post free (£4.95 overseas)

No. 2 **The Air Between, Poems of Clere Parsons (1908-1931)**
Introduced by T.W. Sutherland with an afterword by Edouard Roditi.
Edition of 500 £4.95 post free (£5.95 overseas)

No. 3 **In The Wings** Stories by T.W. Sutherland with a translation of a feuilleton by August Wolf. Illustrated by Fred Fowler.
Edition of 250 £6.95 post free (£7.95 overseas)

No. 4 **Poems of George Oppen (1908-1984)** Selected and introduced by Charles Tomlinson.
Edition of 750 £6.95 post free (£7.95 overseas)

No. 5 **The Journal of an Apprentice Cabbalist** by Edouard Roditi with collages by Michael Thorp.
Edition of 350 £6.95 post free (£7.95 overseas)

Forthcoming contributors to the series will include Elizabeth Smither, James Kirkup, Lawrence Fixel and David Gascoyne.

All orders/enquiries should be addressed to:

The Editor, CLOUD, 48 Biddlestone Road, Heaton, Newcastle upon Tyne NE6 5SL

Volcano Smoke at Diamond Beach
is published in a limited edition
of 350 copies

this is copy number

135